IN

I was born in the Dominican Republic, but my family moved to the United States when I was only eight years old. Now at 35 years-old my husband and I decided to move back with our seven year-old daughter and five year-old son so that we could spend more time together as a family and focus on helping others, among other things.

We have been blessed with a wonderful family and group of friends who have really shown their support for our decision to come here. In fact, several have made the long trip to the island to see us and share the interesting experience of life "in the Dominican." I would like to take this opportunity to thank those who have been able to come and those of you who haven't but have sent cards and love. It has really encouraged us. Thank you.

Now, one of my concerns about moving here was the food. Since this is an under- developed country, I was afraid we would have to lower our standards as far as what we ate. I'm glad to say I was very wrong! The food here is incredible! I find myself asking for recipes all the time because my family and I are loving the Dominican cuisine.

Of course, I have tried all these wonderful recipes on our visitors, and they too want to know how to make it. So I decided to put some of the best ones in this cook book. What I really love about these recipes is that they are all natural. NO ARTIFICIAL INGREDIENTS.

Now, you may be thinking that I live in a beautiful tropical island where everything is laid back and can't possibly relate to you. So, how can I suggest what you should cook? Well, just a year ago, I was a working mom. I worked part-time and home schooled our two children. I know the struggle of putting good-tasting, healthy food on the table in very little time. It wasn't that long ago; I can still feel that angst.

That is precisely why I wrote this book. These recipes are four things: **healthy, quick, simple, and delicious.**

Returning to the island has been very good for me. Before coming, I found myself turning to pre-prepared meals to feed my family due to the limited time available. I simply didn't have time to make a home-cooked meal. Even though I am busy with other things, I haven't had to work for the past year, and so I now have time to cook good meals. Although I have come in touch with my roots since we moved here, I'm still a multi-tasking American mom. So, I've figured out ways to cook healthy quickly, but without sacrificing the flavor.

I use coconut oil for all of the récipes, and I will explain why. Since I was coming to an island replete with coconuts, before I left, I did some research on the subject and found out some wonderful things, especially about coconut oil.

At first, I only used the coconut oil for medicinal reasons. But, a couple of weeks after we got here, we visited Barahona. It is a beautiful town on the south side of the island, along the Caribbean sea. I would try to describe the amazing beauty of this place, but I would fail miserably. So…here's a picture:

We stayed with some friends who were so hospitable; they made us breakfast, lunch, and dinner, which was when my love affair with coconut oil began! She cooked EVERY-THING with coconut oil. Rice, beans, chicken, fish. It was all so incredible! Although we were in a kitchen with a an un-even concrete floor, holes in the tin roof, and could see the sun shining through the wood siding, we felt like we were at a five star restaurant .

In this book, I'm going to show you what I've learned; how to make the best tasting, healthiest food in no time. We'll start with the basics.

THE BASICS

I grew up in The Bronx, New York in an area where many Dominican immigrants live. So, I knew a bit about the culture. One thing that most, if not all, Dominicans in the States use to cook almost everything is *sofrito*. They sauté a spoon full or two of the concoction in some oil and use that to cook the beans or season the rice. They marinade the meat with *sofrito* hours or even days before cooking. The ingredi-ents will vary from one family to another, but this is the basic recipe. You'll notice I say "some" for each ingredient. The amounts depend on how much *sofrito* you would like to make and which seasoning you wish to have stand out.

Sofrito

Some garlic
Some onion
Some cilantro
Some peppers
Some salt
Some lime

Throw it all in the blender and then pour into glass jars. No need to complicate it. It will last you a couple of months. This will save you a lot of time in the long run.

Now that I've told you how to make it and how to use it, I'll tell you that since I have a little more time now, I prefer to prepare my seasoning fresh with each meal. I use the same ingredients, but I mash up the garlic and salt with a mortar and pestle, and chop the onion, pepper, and cilantro.

Rice…

is a staple here. Most Dominicans have rice every day, and it's always fluffy. Here is a sure way to make yours turn out perfect every time.

Always rinse the rice before cooking. Depending on the rice, you may have to rinse more than once. In a sauce pan, pour 2 cups of water for every cup of rice. Let the water come to a boil. Add a pinch of salt, as you would for pasta. Add a tablespoon of oil per 1 cup of rice. Then add your rinsed rice.

Here is a time-honored tradition for you: stir the rice with a spoon, place it in the middle of the pot and see if it will stand up on its own. If it does, then your rice should turn out perfect! This will depend on two factors: the right proportion of rice to water and the right size sauce pan. If it doesn't stand up on its own, you may have to remove a little bit of water.

Leave heat on high until the water is absorbed. At this point, spoon your rice into a mountain in the middle of your pot, put the heat on low and cover your pot for 7-10 minutes. Then, spread the rice out again and cover for another 7-10 minutes. That's all there is to it.

I have used both stainless steel and aluminum pots for this. Leave me a message and let me know how this worked for you at: HealthyCookingWithDominicanFlavor.blogspot.com and get another recipe free.

Beans…

are the other Dominican staple. I guess you can call it stewed beans. I prefer to begin with dried beans. However, for this you would need a pressure cooker or a whole lot of time. If you don't have either of those things, then use canned beans. If you start with the dried beans though, the end result will have been worth the effort. If you get the dried beans (I usually choose pinto, but sometimes black and sometimes white), it is recommended that they soak in water over night. Now, you need to boil them for about an hour in a regular pan or 20 minutes in a pressure cooker.

When your beans are soft, add 3 mashed cloves of garlic, 1 medium onion thinly sliced, a small bunch of cilantro, a ¼ of a small pumpkin cut into 1" cubes, salt to taste, and 2 tablespoons of coconut oil per 2 cups of beans or 2 cans. Let it boil for another five minutes, or until the small pieces of pumpkin are soft. At this point, I like to add some sliced bell pepper and take out ½ a cup of the beans from the pan, blend it and then put it back in the pan and stir for a minute or two. This gives it a hearty consistency. That's it!

MAIN COURSES

Eggplant Casserole

½ cup of flour or corn meal
2 teaspoons of salt divided
2 teaspoons of pepper divided
1 large egg
2 small eggplants
1 lb of ground beef
2 tomatoes diced
3 cloves of garlic mashed
1 bunch of cilantro cut up
½ a small onion diced
1 cup of coconut oil divided
3 cups of shredded mozzarella

For your eggplant: cut length wise thin. Add salt and pepper to eggplant pieces. In a bowl, beat the egg. Put the flour or corn meal on a plate. Dredge the eggplant in the egg then flour. In a frying pan heat some of your coconut oil. Fry the pieces 2 minutes on each side. Remember to cut them thin. Set aside.

For your meat: Add salt and pepper to your ground beef. Fry in a pan with some oil. Add garlic, onion, tomatoes. Cook for 10 minutes.

Assemble your casserole in a 9 inch square pan. One layer of eggplant, then the meat, then another layer of eggplant, then spread a generous amount of mozzarella all over the top. Put it in the oven at 400 degrees for 15 minutes or until cheese melts. Let it sit for 5 minutes. Then enjoy with a tossed salad or rice and beans!

Yields 8 servings

Eggplant casserole fresh out of the oven.

Roasted Chicken with Wasakaka (my version)

The sauce for this recipe was made famous here in the Dominican Republic by a restaurant chain. They don't share the recipe but, it's not hard to figure out. I also added an ingredient of my own and had amazing results. This one takes a little longer, but it's still very easy to make because the oven and the blender do all the work for you. And the result is succulent!

3 lbs chicken
1 tablespoons of salt (divided)
1 tablespoon of dry oregano
2 cloves of garlic
1 small onion
1 teaspoon of lime
1 sour orange

½ cup of water

Preheat your oven to 450° degrees. Thoroughly rinse the chicken with clean water inside and out. Slice the sour orange in half and squeeze the juice all over the chicken. Then rub on the salt (saving some for the sauce) and the oregano. Bake the chicken for an hour.

While that bakes, let's make the Wasakaka. Blend the garlic, onion, lime juice, a pinch of salt, and water.

Your chicken should be turning a nice golden color now. Pull it from the oven and pour the sauce all over and inside the chicken. Place it back in the oven and bake for another 15 minutes. Done!! Succulent is the only way to describe it!

We usually eat this with boiled Yuca (Cassava) covered with sautéed pickled red onion, but if you can't get that, rice and beans are sure to please!

Yields 6 servings

Shrimp Mofongo (Moh fóhn goh)

Mofongo is a Dominican delicacy made with green plantains and a meat of choice; the most common choice being chicharron (fried pork chunks.) My favorite, however, is the shrimp mofongo. You can usually get this when you visit the coast. It tastes heavenly with fresh shrimp, but I've also made it with cooked shrimp, and it's still been very good. I must warn you, this dish is a little more work, but it is well worth it! You'll be transported to a tropical island shore while these flavors dance the merengue in your mouth. (Disclaimer: Any references to food actually dancing are not to be understood as literal.)

3 large green plantains
1 lb of shrimp
4 cloves of garlic
Cilantro chopped
2 large tomatoes
2 tablespoons of olive oil
Coconut oil
½ small onion
1 pinch of salt

Make tostones (under Appetizers-Sides.) Mash 4 cloves of garlic, put half in a small bowl with the olive oil, and set aside.

Blend the tomato, onion, cilantro and pinch of salt, then put it in a small sauce pan with 2 table spoons of coconut oil. Stir sauce just until heated thru.

In a skillet, over high heat, put 2 tablespoons of coconut oil. Sauté the other half of the mashed garlic. Now add your shrimp and cook for 3 minutes, or until it's cooked thru. Immediately remove the shrimp from the skillet and divide them between 4 plates.

Put about 6 tostones in the mortar, dip and re-dip your pestle into the bowl of garlic and olive oil while pounding your tostones and forming them into a hollow ball. Empty the mashed plantain ball directly on top of the shrimp. Repeat this process for all four plates of shrimp. Finally, spoon over some of your tomato sauce on each mound of mashed plantain. Eat right away. Goes great with an ice cold beer!

Locrio de Chuleta

This dish is made with smoked pork chops, but if you can't get any, thick-cut bacon is a savory substitute.

1lb of smoked pork chops
2 cups of rice
2 cloves of garlic
2 small bell peppers (or pepper of your choice)
1 small bunch of cilantro
1tablespoon of Bixa for coloring (also known as Achiote, Lipstick tree, and Annato)
Pinch of salt

Cut the pork chops or bacon into small chunks or slices. Put them in a sauce pan over medium heat. Mash the garlic, pepper, and cilantro in a mortar and pestle, then add to the pork. Once the pork is cooked and has released some oil, throw out about half the oil and keep the other half. Add 4 cups of water to your pot. Let it come to a boil. Add the bixa. **If you can't find bixa where you live, you can substitute with saffron.** Now, follow the instructions for Rice under The Basics. Once the rice is fluffy, you're done!

Dominicans accompany this dish with beans (see *Beans*) and a green salad tossed with homemade dressing: salt, olive oil, pepper and lime juice. You'll no doubt enjoy this dressing more than any you can buy in the grocery store! Best of all, no preservatives!

Yields 6 servings

APPETIZERS — SIDES

Arepita (ah ray péet ah) de Yuca
(Cassava Fritter)

Yuca or Cassava is a starchy root; more firm than a potato. Back in the States, I was able to buy it frozen at Asian stores, but I never had it like this until Laida (the best neighbor in the world) brought me a sample. Of course, I had to know how to make them, and now I share it with the world. (Laida is OK with that.)

2 lbs of Cassava or Yuca
1 clove of garlic
½ a teaspoon of salt
½ teaspoon of pepper
1 sprig of cilantro, chopped
Coconut oil

Shred the cassava and the garlic into a mixing bowl. Add the cilantro, salt, and pepper. Mix it all up with a fork or your fingers. Cover the bottom of your frying pan with the coconut oil. Once your oil is hot, spoon in the mix and flatten. I like to use a wooden spoon. Let fry until golden brown on both sides.

Yields 16 fritters

Tostones (Toh stóh nays)

These are double-fried green plantains.

2 green plantains
Coconut oil
Salt

To peel the plantains, chop off each end and then slice the rind along one of its ridges. You should now be able to remove the rind with relative ease. You might want to use gloves for this process since the plantains secrete a gooey, sticky juice. Now cut the plantain into approximately 1" slices. Cover the bottom of your frying pan with oil. Place the plantains in the pan. Fry them for a minute on each side. Now remove them, press each one with the flat bottom of a cup (I use the bottom of my pestle,) then place them back in the pan. Fry them for another minute or two on each side. I like to put a couple of napkins on the platter where I place the tostones to absorb any excess oil.

When you're done, take away the napkins and top with a little salt. They taste best when eaten warm. So serve'em right away!

Yields 12-14 Tostones

JUICE

I had a huge *aha!* moment (as they say) when it comes to juice drinks. When we first arrived on the island, we went out to eat a few times and enjoyed the most delicious fruit drinks. Pineapple, passion fruit, cherry; they were so good! I wondered how they made them.

Then, it happened! A friend made us a delicious mango drink, sent it with her nephew along with some extra mangos so that we could make some more. Well, like a dummy, I called her and asked, "what do you put in it?" and she said, rather confused, "well, you peel the mango and cut the flesh, put it in the blender and add some water…then, hit the button." I thought, that can't be all, this is so yummy, there must be more to it. But, no, it's just the fruit, some water, depending on how liquid you want it. If the fruit is a little sour you can add some sugar, to taste. And, if you don't want to drink the fibers, then you can strain it.

Freshly blended chinola (passion fruit) juice. You might have to visit to get this one!

We enjoy this amazing, healthy juice all the time. Store-bought juice? Ha! That hasn't been in my house ever since. This juice is wonderful, and I can control how much sugar goes into it. The best part…our six-year-old can pronounce all the ingredients! So, try it with your favorite fruit!! Now, for…

THE COCTAILS

Banana Mama

½ cup of bananas
½ cup of strawberries
½ cup of pineapple
1 cup of coconut milk

Put all of the ingredients in a blender, add sugar to taste, add rum to taste (or make virgin, as a smoothie) add ice to your liking. Strain and pour into cocktail glass.

Yields 4 servings

Coco Loco

1 can of coconut milk
1 can of coconut cream
Ice to your liking
Rum to taste

This drink can be blended or on the rocks, it's tasty either way. If you can find a real coconut to replace the can of coconut milk, even better! It's incredible! Kick the island style up another notch and pour the finished product back into coconut and sip with a straw. Oh so thirsty right now!

Yields 4 servings

Piña Colada

1 cup of pineapple
1 cup of coconut cream
Ice to your liking

Blend all the ingredients, add rum to taste or have virgin as a smoothie. No need to strain; just pour and enjoy!

Yields 4 servings

Cuba Libre (a.k.a. Rum and coke!)

In a glass, put ice cubes, pour rum to taste, and add the Coke. For that island flavor, make sure to squeeze in a little lime and leave the wedge in the glass. Mmmmm!

DESSERTS

Now, I'll be honest with you, Dominicans are known for incredible cooking, but not so much for the desserts. When we first got here, we were taken in at bakeries by the **beautiful -looking** (key word) desserts. We would buy it, take one bite, and then toss it! After a half dozen attempts, we finally gave up on Dominican bakeries. However, there are some very tasty dessert treats to be found here.

I will start with a very typical Dominican dessert, The Flan. You may have had this dessert before and thought it was too eggy or may not have liked the consistency. Well, this recipe takes care of both of those problems. This is actually my husband's recipe. About 15 years ago, he started trying different amounts of the ingredients in traditional flan and added some of his own. For weeks he did this, until he found the perfect recipe.

Every time he makes it, people absolutely love it! When we came here, we figured this would be the real trial since these people know a good flan. So, he made a big batch of flan, took it to a party we were invited to and… it was a hit! Just like back home, our friends here ask him for it all the time. This is a no-fail recipe. So without further ado…

Darian's Flan

1 can of evaporated milk
1can of sweetened condensed milk
3 eggs
1 teaspoon of vanilla
½ block of cream cheese
3 tablespoons of sugar
1/3 cup of water

For the top of your flan: in a pot, put the sugar and the water over high heat and stir. Once the syrup begins to caramelize, turning golden brown in color, turn off the heat. If this is an oven-safe pot, just wait until the syrup cools, if not, quickly pour into an oven-safe pan and make sure you cover the entire bottom of the pan. This is important since you will be flipping your flan and you want a nice golden color on the top. Now preheat oven to 350°.

After the caramelized syrup has cooled, blend the rest of the ingredients and pour into the oven-safe pan.

Place it in the oven for about one hour. Before removing, test flan inserting a clean, dry table knife in the center. If it comes up clean, it is ready. After removing from the oven, separate the edges of the flan from the pan with the knife and allow it to cool to room temperature before putting it in the fridge.

It may not be the prettiest dessert you've made, but it makes up for it in flavor! This dessert is best served chilled.

Candied Plantains

Dominicans don't let anything go to waste. Over-ripe plantains…no problem! There is a very simple recipe for that dilemma.

2 plantains
2 sticks of cinnamon
2 tablespoons of coconut oil
1 tablespoon of sugar

Peel the plantains and cut them in half. Break up the cinnamon sticks and place one piece in each plantain half. In a medium sauce pan, heat the oil and sugar and stir until evenly mixed and then add the plantains. Roll the plantains around so they get completely covered with the mixture. Cover for ten minutes but occasionally stirring. The plantains are a beautiful golden color when they are done. This tasty treat is great on its own but even better a la mode. Mmmmm!   It reminds me of the feeling I get when it's snowing outside, but I get to stay in. You know the feeling?

Pineapple Upside Down Torte

Inspired by the abundance of pineapple here on the island, this is a recipe I absolutely love. In the city, there are produce vendors at all the busy intersections selling ripe, juicy, sweet pineapple. They even come right up to your car with a big smile and their arms full!

You'll notice some resemblance to the pineapple upside down cake, but this is a torte made with real fruit juice and coconut oil instead of butter. The flavor is like…hmmm, how do I describe it? I mean, it has pineapple, coconut, and rum. You get where I'm going with this? YES!! The flavor is like that!

1 medium pineapple cut in half (one half for your topping and one half for the batter)
5 tablespoons of coconut oil (divided)
1 ¾ cups of brown sugar (divided)
¼ tsp salt
1 ½ cups of all-purpose flour
2 teaspoons of baking powder
2 eggs
1 teaspoon of vanilla
2 tablespoons of dark rum

For your topping: take half of your pineapple and cut into any shape of your liking. This will later go on the bottom of your pan (just make sure they are thin slices.) In an iron skillet over medium heat, add the three tablespoons of coconut oil and ¾ cup of brown sugar. Stir until it starts to caramelize and turn a beautiful golden color. Now add your slices of pineapple and let cool.

In a large bowl, sift together the flour, baking powder, and salt. In a separate bowl, with an electric mixer, mix the 2 tablespoons of coconut oil, 1 cup of sugar, eggs, vanilla and rum. Add the flour mixture. In a blender, puree the other half of the pineapple with ½ cup of water and then add half of the juice to your batter. Blend thoroughly. Now pour your batter over the caramelized topping in your iron skillet.

Bake at 350 degrees for 45 minutes. After removing from the oven, let the torte stand for 5 minutes. With a butter knife, separate the edges of the torte from the skillet. Place a serving dish upside down over the skillet, then carefully turn over allowing the torte to fall on the dish. If any pineapple sticks to the pan, just remove it with a spatula and put back on the torte. Enjoy!

Above: Caramelizing the coconut oil and brown sugar

Fresh-cut pineapple wedges placed on top of caramelized mixture.

Pouring batter onto the pineapple topping.

Fresh out of the oven. Just needs to be flipped over onto your favorite dessert platter.

Well, I've certainly enjoyed telling you about these great recipes. Talking about food is definitely at the top of my list of favorite subjects. I'm anxious for you to try them and enjoy them with your friends and family. There's nothing more satisfying than your loved ones making sounds like: mmmm, ohhhh, uh huh, and that's what I'm talkin about! Get used to it; you'll being hearing a lot of it!

Thank you for purchasing the book. I would love to hear back from you. Tell me which of the recipes was a big hit at your house. You can also check out our Facebook page for new recipes and cooking tips or even have updated information and recipes tweeted to you. All the links are posted below.

Healthy Cooking with Dominican Flavor

Healthy Cooking with Dominican Flavor
http://HealthyCookingWithDominicanFlavor.blogspot.com

Made in the USA
Coppell, TX
06 December 2019

12448963R00017